This book belongs to...

The Twilight Fairies

Illustrated by

Margaret W. Tarrant

Original poetry by

Marion St. John Webb

Series Editor

Fiona Waters

First published in this format in 2002 by
The Medici Society Ltd
Grafton House, Hyde Estate Road, London NW9 6JZ

Copyright © The Medici Society Ltd 2002 / 1928

First published in 1928 by The Medici Society Ltd
3 5 7 9 10 8 6 4 2

A catalogue record for this book is available from the British Library.

ISBN 0 85503 260 X

Margaret Tarrant's original artworks have been rescanned for this re-designed edition.

Designed by Tony Potter Publishing Ltd

Printed in Singapore

The
Twilight Fairies

Contents

M W Tarrant

The Fairies' Hour

Outside the window of the little house
The fairies hide upon the window-sill.
"This is our hour," they sing, "for fairies still
Are needed in the twilight of the day."
Wherever children are, the fairies stay,
And listen at the window or the door.
Outside the window of the little house
The fairies wait once more.

Inside the window of the little house
The children are in bed, but not asleep.
The watching fairies nod, and closer creep
To listen while the children's mother sings
A tale of gentle dreams and fairy things.
And when the story's ended, just for a while,
  Outside the window of the little house
        The fairies sit and smile.

Outside the window of the little house
The fairies dance upon the window-sill.
"This is our hour," they sing,"for children still
Believe in us and say that we are real.
We shall make magic they can feel
For every child who waves a hand,
    Outside the window of the house
        Look! Here is Fairyland!"

Sing a Song of Starlight

Sing a song of fairies
  Dancing through the trees.
Somebody is yawning,
Is it dreamtime, please?

Not until the fairies put a glow-worm
  in a jar,
And fly up through the dusk, my dear,
  And light the evening star.

Sing a song of starlight.
For the dreams are here.
Now somebody is waking,
Is the morning here?

Not until the fairies finish polishing the sun,
And fly up to the stars, my dear,
And blow out every one.

A Fairy Passes By

All flowers close their petals
When the twilight falls,
But will open up again
If a fairy calls.

To have a minute's gossip
No fairy can refuse,
And every little flower that grows
Likes a bit of news.

So if you see a nodding flower
At the end of day,
You will most surely know
A fairy's passed that way.

Margaret W Tarrant

An Unwanted Lullaby

Lullaby, lullaby, little blue bird.
 Gently the bough we're swinging.
Shut both your eyes like a good little bird,
And listen to fairies singing.

Lullaby, lullaby . . .
What is it *now?*
Somebody's pushing you right off the bough?
Nobody's pushing, it's only the breeze,
Whispering here in the tops of the trees!

Lullaby, lullaby, little blue bird.
Brightly the stars are gleaming.
Do go to sleep like a good little bird,
And sweetly you'll soon be dreaming.

Lullaby, lullaby . . .
What did you say?
Can't go to sleep while we make the
  bough sway?
Don't like our singing, it's the worst
  you have heard?
Oh! What a naughty, ungrateful
  blue bird!

The Ugly Signpost

"Twenty miles to London,"
The signpost it read.
"What an ugly signpost,"
Everybody said.
Dirty, scratched and broken
In the light of day,
Everybody laughed at it
As they passed that way.

But at dusk the twilight
Gently floated down,
All around the signpost
Twenty miles from town.
Through the dusk it glimmered,
White against the tree.
Beautiful and graceful
Then it seemed to be.

Dancing round it happily,
Swinging on its arm,
Fairies in the twilight
Found it full of charm.
"Twenty miles to London,"
All the fairies read.
"What a lovely signpost,"
All the fairies said.

So each ugly signpost
Has its special hour,
Waiting through the daytime
For the magic power
That will come at twilight.
And then things old and plain
Shall be touched with beauty,
And all grow young again.

The Thief

"Why does the Dawn creep up
     With her face so grey
  and pale?
Surely she should come
Smiling, without fail.
She is the special one,"
The Twilight Fairies say.
"For to the world she brings
Every brand new day."

Here is the creeping Dawn
With face so pale and grey.
"Oh," she says, "how I wish
That night might always stay
Over the sleeping land.
For then I would not stray
Into the world to steal
All pleasant dreams away."

Margaret Winifred Tarrant (1888 - 1959)

'Every time a child says, " I don't believe in fairies," ' warned Peter Pan, 'there is a little fairy somewhere that falls down dead.' By her paintings Margaret Tarrant did as much to encourage children's belief in fairies as J M Barrie did by his writings. Born in London in 1888, the only child of artist Percy Tarrant and his wife Sarah, Margaret excelled at art from an early age, and she was only 19 when she received her first, very prestigious, commission, from J M Dent & Sons: to illustrate Charles Kingsley's much-loved children's classic, *The Water Babies*, which was first published in 1863.

Her delicate, charming pictures matched the spirit of the story perfectly and earned her a string of new commissions: *Nursery Rhymes* (1914 and 1923), *Alice in Wonderland* (1916) and

Hans Andersen's Fairy Tales (1917) for Ward Lock & Co., plus postcards for Oxford University Press.

Margaret Tarrant illustrated some 20 books for George G. Harrap & Co. between 1915 and 1929, but an even more important publishing relationship began in 1920, when she completed her first pieces for The Medici Society. This was to prove a long and fruitful connection, resulting in most of her best-known work. In the 1920s, for example, she illustrated this highly successful series of fairy books for the company, written by the poet and author Marion St John Webb. Her picture of Peter's Friends, inspired by J M Barrie's *Peter Pan* stories and the statue in Kensington Gardens, proved so popular when it appeared in 1921 that it had to be reproduced many times.

Peter's Friends

The dusk of the nineteenth and dawn of the twentieth centuries were magical times for fairy lovers. Fascination with fairy lore was widespread, reaching unprecedented heights in 1922 when Sir Arthur Conan Doyle published *The Coming of the Fairies*, containing 'photographs' of fairies taken by two young girls in a Yorkshire village, which were later proved to be hoaxes. The story was actually a fascinating deception, which was believed by many reputable people. The mystery was not solved until towards the end of the twentieth century, when the girls involved, now elderly ladies, explained what had really happened.

In 1922, Margaret Tarrant's *Do You Believe in Fairies?* showed two children encircled by a ring of fairies, which caught the public excitement already created by Sir Arthur Conan Doyle's book.

Do You Believe in Fairies?

This interest was mirrored in an outpouring of art and literature. Children's books cultivated belief in fairies: they were used in religious teaching, magazines were devoted to them, and captivating new works appeared, most notably J M Barrie's *Peter Pan* and *Peter Pan in Kensington Gardens*. Rudyard Kipling wrote *Rewards and Fairies* and even Beatrix Potter embraced the subject in *The Fairy Caravan*.

Artists revelled in the
opportunity to portray
imaginary worlds. Arthur
Rackham, the most fashionable
illustrator of his day, depicted a
sinister fantasy landscape,
peopled by spiky goblins, fairies
and mice amid gnarled trees with gnomelike
faces. In contrast, Honor Appleton, Maud Tindal
Atkinson and Mabel Lucie Atwell offered gentler,
comforting images recalling Kate Greenaway's
illustrations of apple-cheeked children.

Margaret Tarrant was one of those most associated
with the depiction of fairies in the 1920s and
1930s, together with her friend and sketching
partner, Cicely Mary Barker (1895 - 1973). Both
began to use Art Nouveau and Arts and Crafts

elements in their work, and in Tarrant's paintings a breathtaking attention to detail - diaphanous wings with the intricate tracery of a dragonfly's wings - is a testament to the reality of fairies, imaginary or otherwise.

During her life Margaret Tarrant tackled a wide range of subjects and won special acclaim for those, such as *All Things Wise and Wonderful*, with a religious theme. But her forte was fairies, for in her evocation of these ethereal figures she could express her love for children, wild flowers and dance, of all that was beautiful and pure.

She would sketch meticulously from life to capture the likeness of a child or plant, then compose her pictures by arranging the subjects in imaginary settings, infusing them with a distinctive otherworldly quality.

Margaret Tarrant's fairies have a unique fluidity and balletic grace that expressed her delight in the free-flowing dance invented by Isadora Duncan. She was very much a free spirit herself, flying along the country lanes around her home in Surrey on an ancient bicycle, leaping off impulsively to sketch a flower or help a toddler to paint. She never married, but she attracted many friends by her generosity, energy and zest for life. Perhaps it was this childlike enthusiasm and innocence, combined with a special kind of imagination, that gave her a natural affinity with fairies.

Much missed when she died in 1959, Margaret Tarrant left a lasting legacy in charming pictures that seem as fresh today as the day they were painted, and still enchant new generations with their glimpses into a secret fairy world.

The Lily Pool

The new edition

There are 12 beautiful fairy books by Margaret Tarrant, originally published between 1923 - 1928. The re-designed edition is now available to collect as a set, with modern scanning methods used to bring out the exquisite detail of the original paintings and drawings.

WATER FAIRIES — WATER FAIRIES

TWILIGHT FAIRIES — TWILIGHT FAIRIES

WEATHER FAIRIES — WEATHER FAIRIES

ORCHARD FAIRIES — ORCHARD FAIRIES

FRUIT FAIRIES — WILD FRUIT FAIRIES

INSECT FAIRIES — INSECT FAIRIES

HOUSE FAIRIES — HOUSE FAIRIES

FOREST FAIRIES — FOREST FAIRIES

SEED FAIRIES — SEED FAIRIES

SEASHORE FAIRIES — SEASHORE FAIRIES

FLOWER FAIRIES — FLOWER FAIRIES

HEATH FAIRIES — HEATH FAIRIES